CFA Institute

CFA INSTITUTE INDUSTRY GUIDES

THE MACHINERY INDUSTRY

by Anthony M. Fiore, CFA

978-0-938367-79-6
September 2013

ABOUT THE AUTHOR

Anthony M. Fiore, CFA, is a senior vice president at Silvercrest Asset Management Group and a research analyst for the firm's equity portfolios. Prior to joining Silvercrest, he was a senior equity analyst at Standard & Poor's, where he covered the machinery, industrial conglomerates, and diversified commercial services industries. Previously, Mr. Fiore was a generalist equity analyst and portfolio manager at State Street Global Advisors in the firm's Global Fundamental Strategies Group. He received a BS in business administration from the University of Vermont with a concentration in finance.

CONTENTS

INDUSTRY OVERVIEW

The machinery industry is composed of a diverse array of end markets and products, including construction and earth-moving equipment, farm machinery, heavy duty trucks, pumps, valves, motors, compressors, hydraulics, filtration, industrial controls, and automation systems, as well as machine tools for cutting, stamping, and forming metal. Most companies operating in the machinery industry are subject to derived demand and experience an increase (decrease) in sales and profits in response to an increase (decrease) in economic activity, industrial production, commodity prices, and/or other factors. Because of the diverse nature of the industry, the primary drivers of demand vary across end markets. Still, companies may be broadly grouped into the four segments shown in **Exhibit 1**.

Exhibit 1.

Although demand for most companies within the machinery industry is influenced by changes in the level of economic activity, certain drivers of demand are unique to each group.

Industry Segment	Key Drivers of Demand
Construction and Mining Equipment	Construction activity; mined commodity prices.
Farm Machinery	Farm income; agricultural commodity prices.
Heavy Trucks	Freight activity; environmental emission regulations.
Industrial Machinery	Manufacturing activity; industrial production.

INDUSTRY STRUCTURE

The industry has a wide variety of companies and end markets. Thus, to get a clear understanding of the overall machinery industry, it is useful to examine the structure of each industry segment.

CONSTRUCTION AND MINING EQUIPMENT

Based on the combined revenues of the world's five largest public construction and mining equipment companies, which in aggregate represent an estimated 60% of total industry revenue, the global construction and mining equipment market was USD148 billion in 2012 (see **Figure 1**).

Industry revenue, as represented by this same group of public companies, has increased at a compound annual growth rate (CAGR) of 15.7% over the past 10 years, largely driven by growing demand in emerging markets, most notably China, which has grown from an estimated 6% of total demand in 2002 to an estimated 31% in 2012 (see **Figures 2a** and **2b**).

A key driver of demand for construction equipment is construction activity, which, in turn, is influenced by global economic activity. Similarly, mining activity is a key driver of demand for mining equipment, which, in turn, tends to be strongly correlated with mined commodity prices—particularly iron ore, coal, and copper prices—which are also influenced by economic activity.

Figure 1. Global Construction and Mining Equipment Market

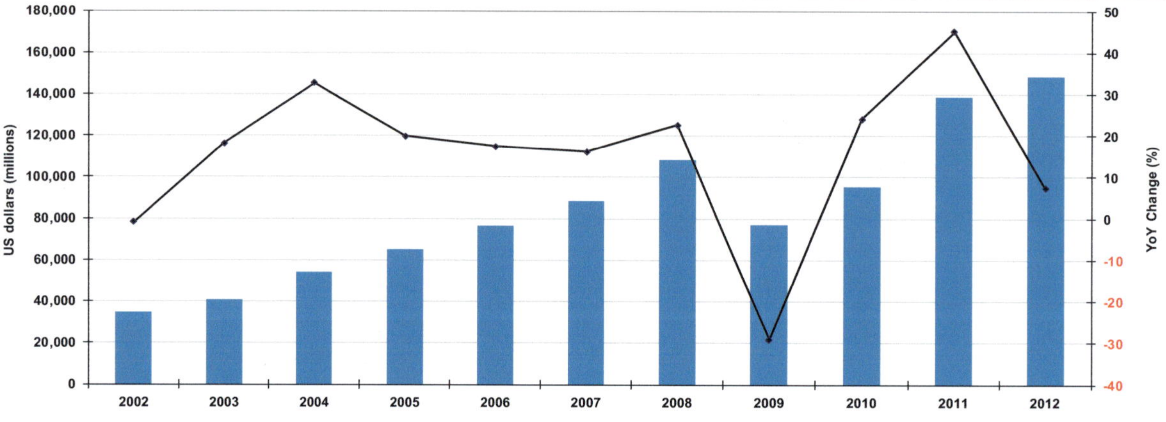

Sources: Company reports; author estimates.

Figure 2a. Estimated 2002 Global Sales by Region

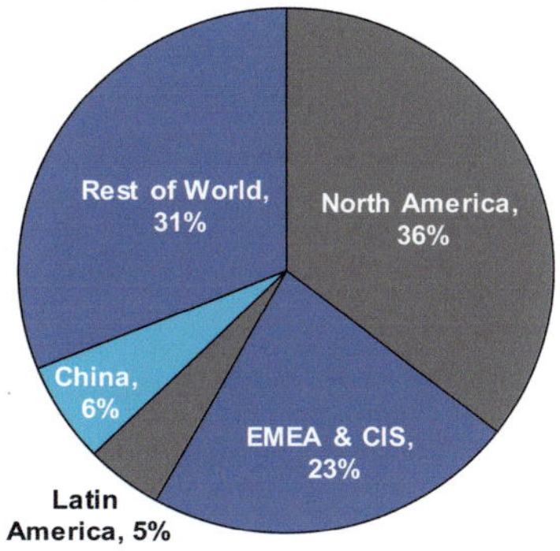

Note: EMEA = Europe, Middle East, and Africa; CIS = Commonwealth of Independent States (an alliance made up of states that had been Soviet Socialist Republics in the Soviet Union prior to its dissolution in December 1991).

Sources: Company reports; author estimates.

Figure 2b. Estimated 2012 Global Sales by Region

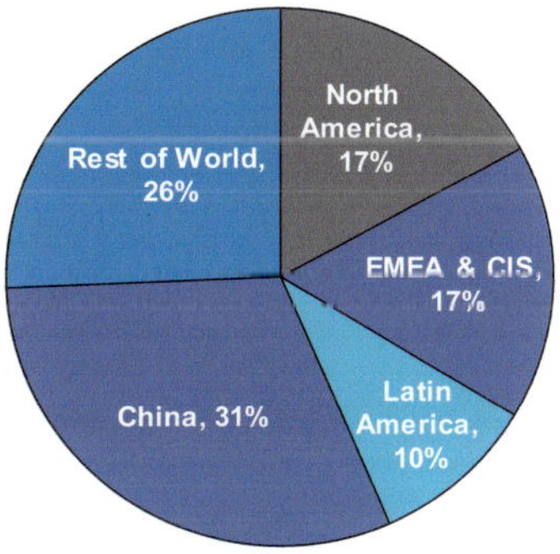

Note: EMEA = Europe, Middle East, and Africa; CIS = Commonwealth of Independent States (an alliance made up of states that had been Soviet Socialist Republics in the Soviet Union prior to its dissolution in December 1991).

Sources: Company reports; author estimates.

One of the better economic indicators that can be used to gauge the health of the construction equipment market in the United States is gross private domestic fixed investment (GPDFI), which is published quarterly by the Bureau of Economic Analysis. GPDFI measures spending by private businesses, nonprofit institutions, and households on fixed assets in the U.S. economy. As **Figure 3** shows, GPDFI is a strong indicator of construction equipment demand, with a correlation of greater than 70% with Caterpillar's retail sales of machinery in North America. Moreover, GPDFI as a percentage of gross domestic product (GDP) has averaged 15.3% since 1947, with a standard deviation of 1.4%, yielding a range of 13.9% to 16.7% (see **Figure 4**). As of December 2012, GPDFI as a percentage of GDP was 13.0%, or more than one standard deviation below the long-term average of 15.3% (Figure 4).

Turning to the companies, Caterpillar is the market share leader within the construction and mining equipment segment and is nearly twice the size of its next largest competitor, Komatsu. A ranking of the five largest public construction equipment companies based on 2012 revenue is provided in **Figure 5**. Other companies

Figure 3. GPDFI and Caterpillar Retail Sales

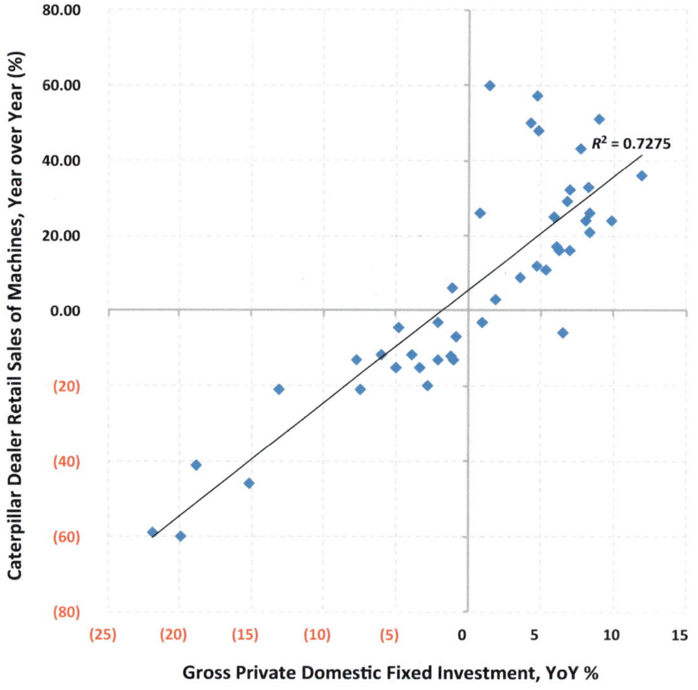

Sources: Bureau of Economic Analysis; company reports.

Figure 4. Gross Private Domestic Fixed Investment as a Percentage of GDP

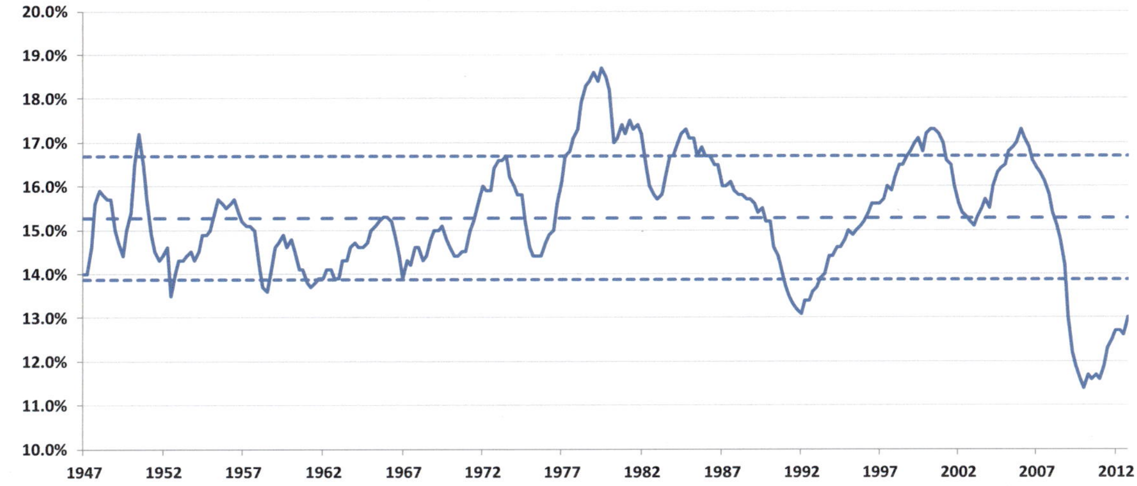

Source: Bureau of Economic Analysis.

Figure 5. Estimated Market Share (based on 2012 revenue)

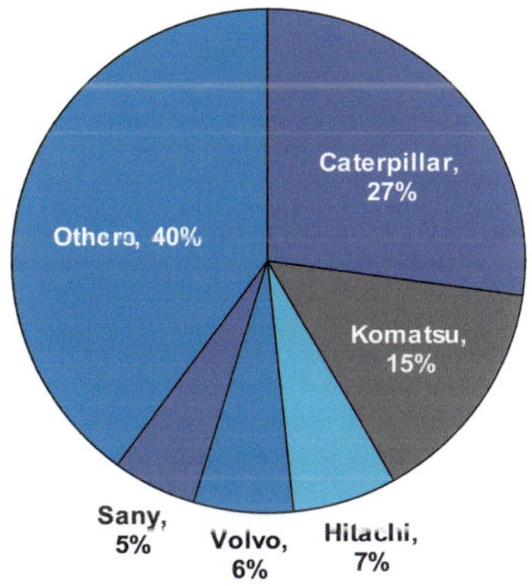

Sources: Company reports; author estimates.

that are similar in size, with about 5% market share each, include China's second largest construction equipment maker Zoomlion; privately owned Liebherr Group, Europe's second largest construction equipment company; Terex, the number two U.S. construction equipment manufacturer; and Doosan Infracore, South Korea's largest equipment maker.

Major product categories within the segment include hydraulic excavators and wheel loaders, which together represent more than 80%, on average, of construction equipment unit volumes (see **Figure 6**).

Figure 6. Demand by Equipment Type [Composition Ratio]

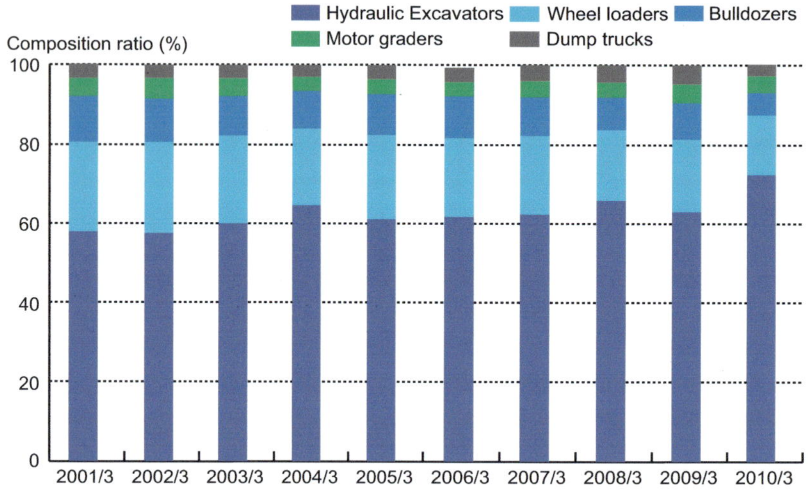

Source: Komatsu Ltd.

FARM MACHINERY

Based on the combined revenues of the world's four largest public manufacturers of farm machinery, which in aggregate represent an estimated 60% of total industry revenue, the global agricultural equipment market was approximately USD104 billion in 2012 (see **Figure 7**).

Industry revenue, as represented by this same group of public companies, has increased at a CAGR of 10.8% over the past 10 years, reflecting a decade of strong growth in cash receipts to farmers (see **Figure 8**).

Although the market for farm equipment is global in nature, the level of mechanization varies among regions, most notably between developed and developing markets (see **Figure 9**).

As illustrated in **Figure 10**, Europe and North America represented slightly more than two-thirds of global demand for agricultural equipment in 2012.

As mentioned earlier, key drivers of demand for agricultural equipment are farm cash receipts, which, in turn, are influenced by crop and livestock prices and government support programs. As shown in **Table 1a**, cash receipts to farmers in the United States were at a record level in 2012, at USD402.1 billion, which was 24% above the long-term trend of USD325 billion.

Figure 7. Global Agricultural Equipment Market

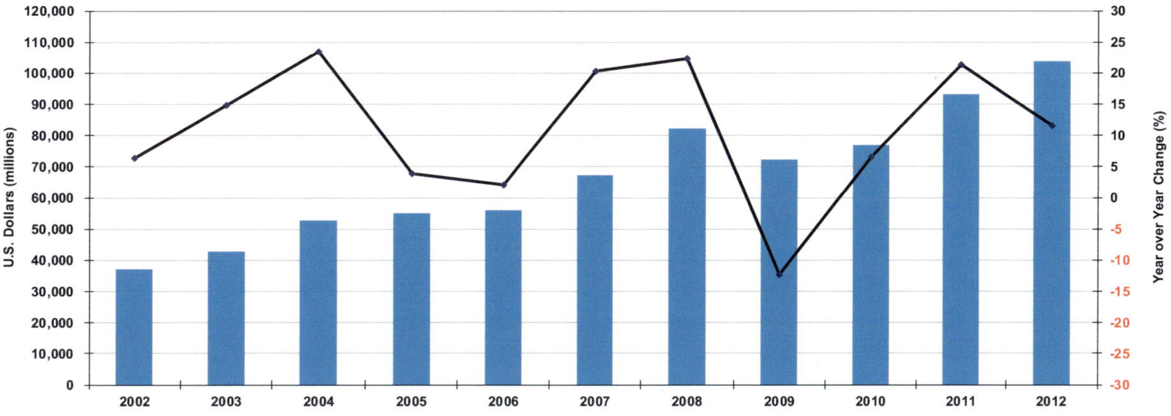

Sources: Company reports; author estimates.

Figure 8. U.S. Cash Receipts from Farming Operations (in billions of U.S. dollars)

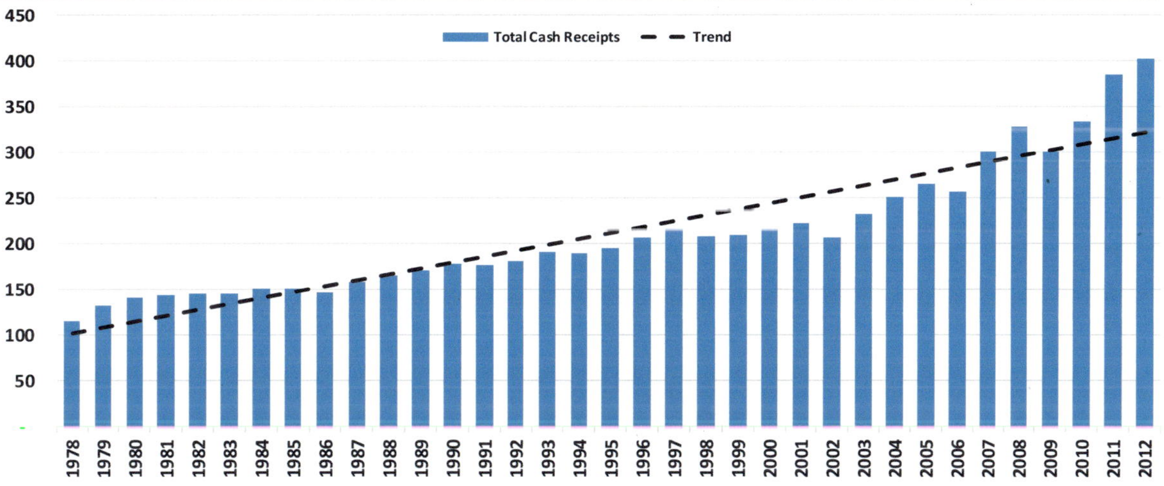

Source: USDA.

Cash receipts (including direct government payments) are a strong indicator of agricultural equipment demand, with a correlation of better than 75% for high horsepower tractors (over 100hp) and combines (see **Table 1b**).

Figure 9. Mechanization Level Comparison (# tractors per 1,000 ag workers)

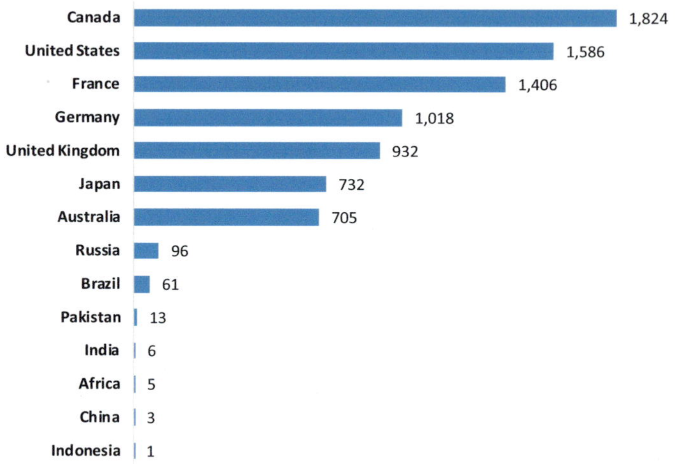

Source: World Development Indicators, World Bank.

Figure 10. Estimated 2012 Global Sales by Region

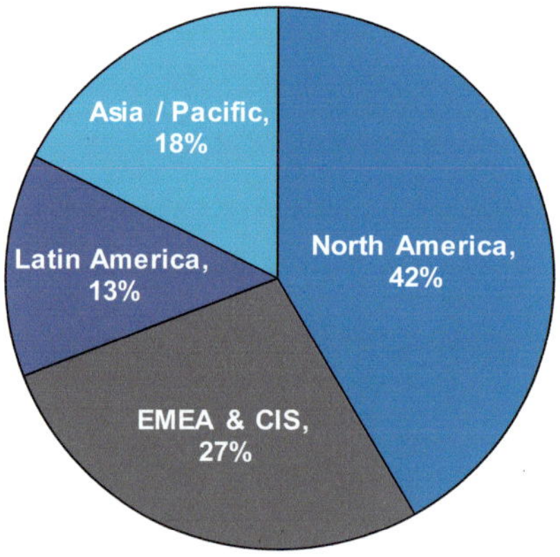

Sources: Company reports; author estimates.

Table 1a. U.S. Farm Cash Receipts (in billions of U.S. dollars)

Year	Crop Receipts	Livestock Receipts	Cash Receipts	Gov't Receipts	Total Cash Receipts	YoY % Change
2000	92.5	99.6	192.1	23.2	215.3	2.9%
2001	93.4	106.7	200.0	22.4	222.5	3.3%
2002	100.7	93.9	194.6	12.4	207.0	–6.9%
2003	110.3	105.7	216.0	16.5	232.5	12.3%
2004	114.4	123.5	237.9	13.0	250.8	7.9%
2005	116.0	124.9	240.9	24.4	265.3	5.8%
2006	122.1	118.5	240.6	15.8	256.4	–3.3%
2007	150.1	138.5	288.5	11.9	300.4	17.2%
2008	175.0	141.6	316.7	12.2	328.9	9.5%
2009	168.9	120.3	289.1	12.2	301.3	–8.4%
2010	179.6	141.6	321.1	12.4	333.5	10.7%
2011	208.3	166.0	374.3	10.4	384.7	15.3%
2012	219.6	171.7	391.2	10.8	402.1	4.5%

Sources: USDA; Association of Equipment Manufacturers.

Table 1b. U.S. Unit Sales of Tractors & Combines

	R^2 = 0.93		R^2 = 0.88		R^2 = 0.78	
Year	>100HP	YoY%	4WD	YoY%	Combines	YoY%
2000	15,647	–0.2%	3,081	–1.0%	5,660	8.8%
2001	17,063	9.0%	3,425	11.2%	6,422	9.1%
2002	13,799	–19.1%	2,680	–21.8%	5,038	1.5%
2003	14,234	3.2%	2,823	5.3%	4,631	20.9%
2004	19,838	39.4%	3,593	27.3%	6,666	12.5%
2005	19,771	–0.3%	3,638	1.3%	6,733	–0.8%
2006	16,643	–15.8%	2,986	–17.9%	6,168	–4.0%
2007	20,875	25.4%	3,657	22.5%	7,104	0.5%
2008	26,261	25.8%	4,427	21.1%	8,464	–9.5%
2009	22,863	–12.9%	4,512	1.9%	9,690	–21.4%
2010	26,971	18.0%	5,784	28.2%	10,678	6.2%
2011	27,427	1.7%	5,977	3.3%	9,898	1.8%
2012	31,732	15.7%	6,935	16.0%	9,820	10.2%

Sources: USDA; Association of Equipment Manufacturers.

Other factors that can influence demand for farm machinery include the financial health of the farmer, used equipment prices, and certain dealer and/or government incentives. Farm balance sheets, as measured by debt-to-asset ratios, are a good indicator of the financial health of farmers (see **Figure 11**). In the United States, farm balance sheets have remained in good shape since the early 1990s. At the end of 2012, they were near the healthiest levels seen in over 50 years.

Used equipment prices can also influence demand. In general, high used equipment prices tend to be supportive of new equipment sales; farmers are increasingly likely to trade in their older equipment toward the purchase of new equipment when used equipment prices are high. Other factors that can influence demand include certain types of incentives, such as dealer financing programs and government-sponsored incentives (e.g., accelerated depreciation tax programs).[1]

Deere & Company is the market share leader within the farm machinery segment and is nearly twice the size of its next largest competitor, CNH Global. A ranking of the four largest public agricultural equipment companies based on 2012 revenue is provided in **Figure 12**. CLAAS Group, a privately owned German company, is estimated to be the fifth largest industry player, with an estimated 4% share of the global market.

The major product categories within the farm machinery segment are high horsepower tractors (> 100HP) and self-propelled combines, which together represented just over half of total U.S. farm machinery sales in 2012 (see **Figure 13**).

Figure 11. Debt-to-Asset Ratio of the U.S. Farming Sector

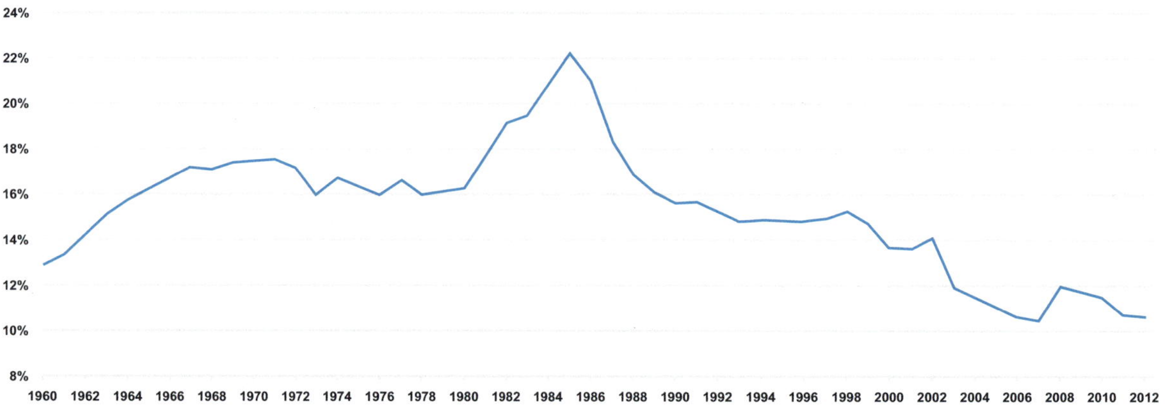

Source: USDA.

[1]Section 179 of the U.S. Internal Revenue Code is an example of a government-sponsored incentive that has helped stimulate demand for farm equipment in recent years. This depreciation deduction allows a taxpayer to deduct the cost of certain types of property as an expense rather than capitalizing the cost of the property and depreciating it over a period of time.

Figure 12. Estimated Market Share (based on 2012 revenue)

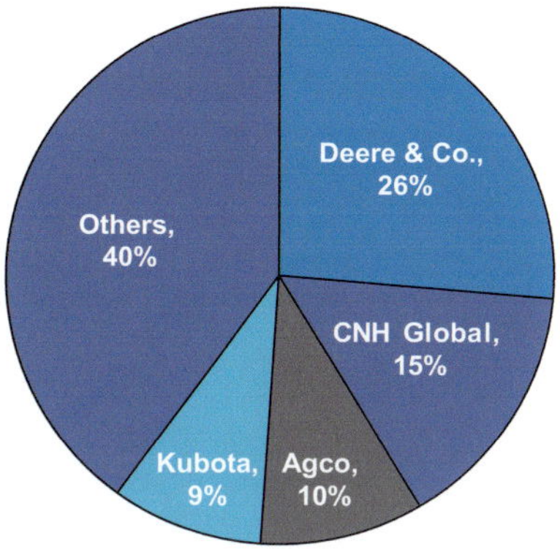

Sources: Company reports; author estimates.

Figure 13. Estimated Sales Mix of U.S. Farm Machinery

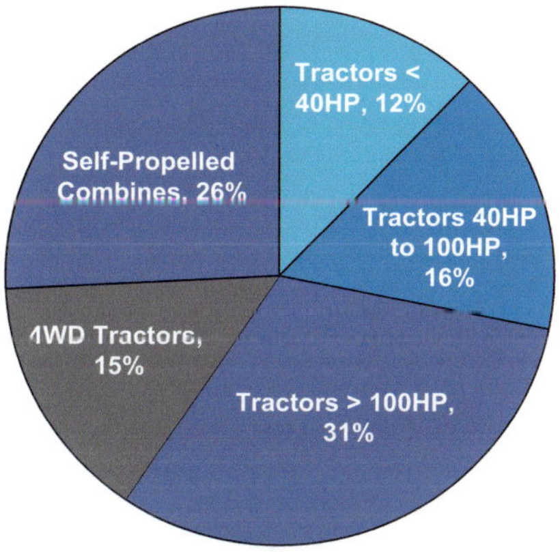

Sources: Association of Equipment Manufacturers; author estimates.

Less than 40HP Tractor Average Sales Price (ASP) $10–30K

40–100HP Utility Tractor ASP $15–75K

More than 100HP ASP USD100–200K

Self-Propelled Combine Harvester ASP USD300–500K

HEAVY TRUCKS

Based on the combined revenues of the world's five largest manufacturers of heavy trucks, which in aggregate represent an estimated 55% of total industry revenue, the global heavy truck market was approximately USD200 billion in 2012 (see **Figure 14**).

Industry revenue, as represented by this same group of public companies, has increased at a compound annual growth rate of 6.8% over the past 10 years, of which we estimate that approximately 40% of the growth (~3% per annum) has been driven by rising prices of equipment, with the remainder of the growth reflecting higher unit volumes. Most of the growth in pricing reflects the increased costs of filtration components and equipment needed to comply with various governmental emission standards, primarily in Europe and North America.

From a regional perspective, the heavy truck market is highly consolidated, with a small number of manufacturers accounting for a high percentage of each regional heavy truck market. For example, in Europe the top six heavy truck manufacturers make up about 95% of the European market, whereas in North America the top four original equipment manufacturers (OEMs) have a collective market share in excess of 95%. In Japan, nearly 90% of the heavy truck market is dominated by just three domestic manufacturers. The Chinese market is the least consolidated of the major regional markets and, similar to Japan, is primarily served by domestic manufacturers, of which the top five collectively control about 80% of China's heavy truck market. **Figures 15a** and **15b** illustrate the estimated mix of sales by region and a ranking of the five largest public manufacturers of heavy trucks based on 2012

Figure 14. Global Heavy Truck Market

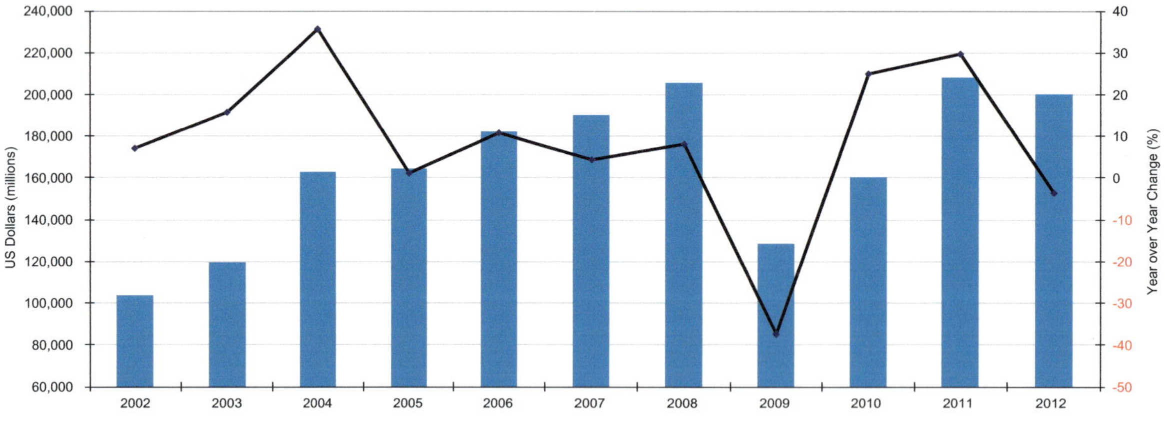

Sources: Company reports; author estimates.

Figure 15a. Estimated 2012 Global Heavy Truck Sales by Region

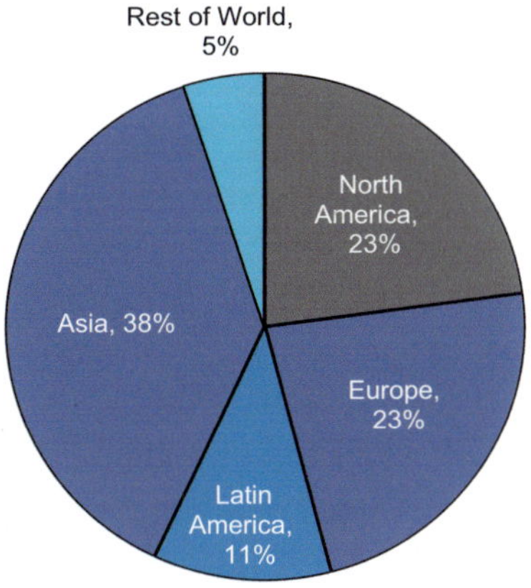

Sources: Company reports; author estimates.

Figure 15b. Estimated Market Share (based on 2012 revenue)

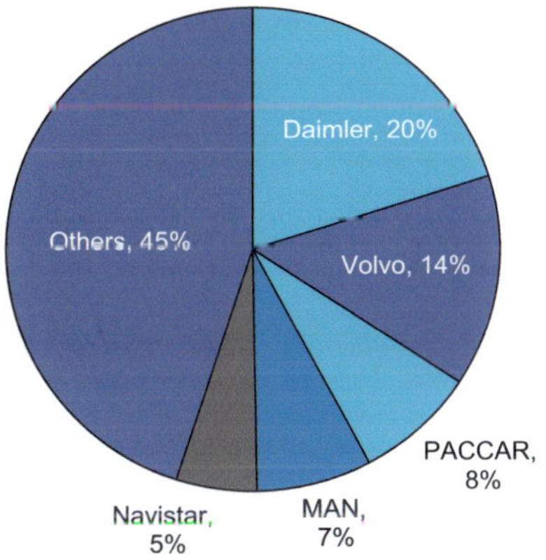

Sources: Company reports; author estimates.

revenue. Daimler is the clear market share leader within the heavy truck segment, with brands that include Mercedes-Benz, Freightliner, Mitsubishi Fuso, and Western Star. Large regional manufacturers include China's Dongfeng Motor Corporation, First Auto Works, and China National Heavy Duty Truck Group; Japan's Isuzu and Hino (a subsidiary of Toyota); India's Tata and Ashok Leyland; and South Korea's Hyundai, which holds approximately 85% of South Korea's heavy truck business.

A key driver of demand for the heavy truck market is trucking activity, which, in turn, is broadly influenced by economic activity, most notably retail sales. A commonly used indicator to measure trucking activity in the United States is the American Trucking Associations (ATA) Tonnage Index. The index is calculated each month based on responses from ATA membership about the amount of tonnage each carrier hauled. The ATA membership sample includes an array of trucking companies, ranging from small fleets to large carriers. As **Figure 16** shows, declines in trucking activity have historically coincided with downturns in the U.S. economy. Figure 16 also shows a 93% correlation between the ATA Tonnage Index and retail sales activity.

In the United States, a commercial truck's classification is determined by the vehicle's weight, with Class 8 representing the heaviest category (see **Table 2**). The main product categories within the heavy truck segment are medium-duty trucks (Class 5–7; 16,001 lbs to 33,000 lbs) and heavy duty trucks (Class 8; over 33,000 lbs).

It is worth mentioning that truck data frequently differ among various industry sources (including the companies themselves). For example, bus and RV data may

Figure 16.

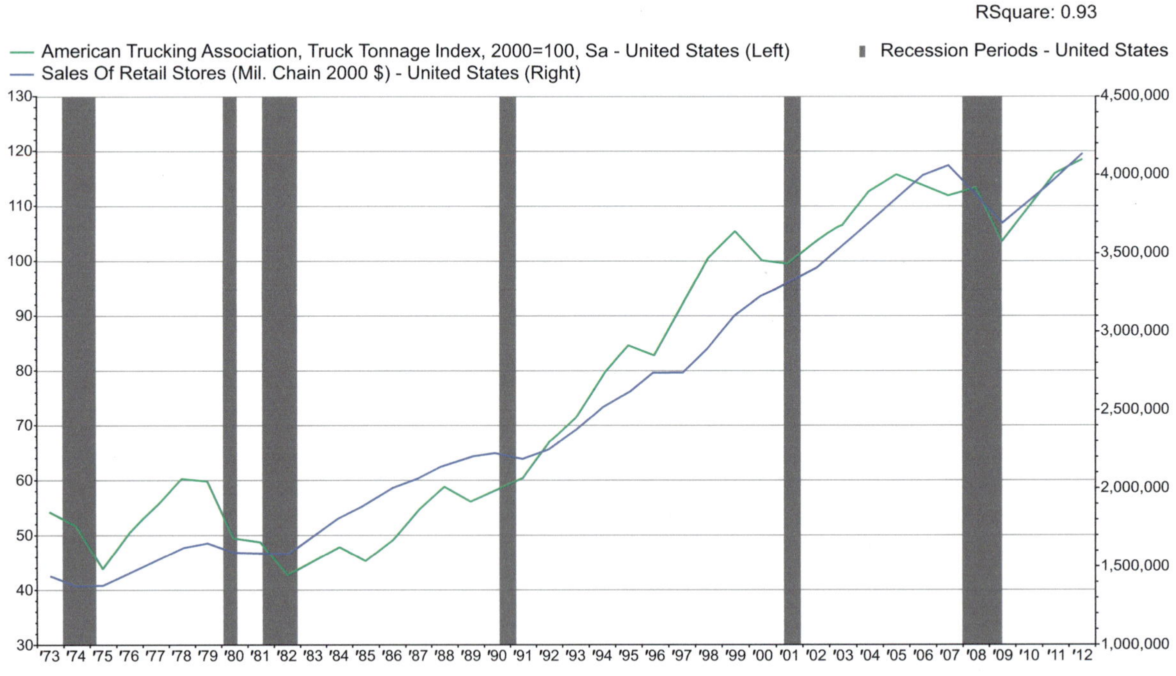

Source: FactSet.

Table 2. Gross Vehicle Weight Ratings

Class	Weight (lbs)	
Class 1	Up to 6,000	
Class 2	6,001–10,000	
Class 3	10,001–14,000	
Class 4	14,001–16,000	
Class 5	16,001–19,500	"Heavy Truck" Segment
Class 6	19,501–26,000	"Heavy Truck" Segment
Class 7	26,001–33,000	"Heavy Truck" Segment
Class 8	33,001 and over	"Heavy Truck" Segment

Source: U.S. DOT Vehicle Inventory and Use Survey 2012.

Class 8 Truck (Typical ASP USD125–135K)

sometimes be included with truck data, although the impact is usually small. Geography can also present its own set of challenges because the truck OEMs often parse their sales data differently. For example, some OEMs might include Mexico in North America, and others might categorize it as part of Latin America.

INDUSTRIAL MACHINERY

This segment is composed of industrial machinery companies whose business operations are not dominated by any of the three segments previously discussed. This group of companies includes a variety of manufacturers whose broad range of products include, but are not limited to, pumps, valves, motors, compressors, hydraulics, filtration, industrial controls, and automation systems, as well as machine tools for cutting, stamping, and forming metal.

Most of the companies operating in the industrial machinery segment are subject to derived demand and will experience an increase (decrease) in their business levels in response to an increase (decrease) in overall manufacturing activity. One of the more salient economic indicators that can be used to track manufacturing activity in the United States is the Institute for Supply Management (ISM) Manufacturing Report on Business.

The ISM Manufacturing Report on Business is one of the timeliest economic indicators that can be used to gauge the health of the industrial machinery segment. Published at 10AM EST on the first business day of each month, it is the first monthly report to focus on activity in the manufacturing sector of the economy during the prior month. ISM computes a composite index measure called the PMI (prior to 2001 the acronym PMI stood for Purchasing Managers Index) based on the survey responses from purchasing managers with regard to manufacturing activity. The PMI is a composite index based on the diffusion indices of five equally weighted indicators, including new orders, production, employment, supplier deliveries, and inventories.[2] A PMI index more than 50 represents growth or expansion within the

[2]A diffusion index measures the degree to which a change in something is dispersed, spread out, or "diffused" in a particular group. If all members of a group of people (sample population) are asked if something has changed and in which direction, they will answer in one of three ways: It has not changed, it has increased, or it has decreased. This is the nature of the ROB (Report on Business) questions.

All the ISM indices are "diffusion indexes" and are indicators of month-to-month change. The percentage response to the "Better," "Same," or "Worse" question is difficult to compare with prior periods; therefore, we diffuse the percentages for this purpose. A diffusion index indicates the degree to which the indicated change is dispersed or diffused throughout the sample population. Respondents to ISM surveys indicate each month whether particular activities (e.g., new orders) for their organizations have increased, decreased, or remained unchanged from the previous month. The ISM indices are calculated by taking the percentage of respondents that report that the activity has increased ("Better") and adding it to one-half of the percentage that report the activity has not changed ("Same") and adding the two percentages. Using half of the "Same" percentage effectively measures the bias toward a positive (above 50%) or negative index. As an example of calculating a diffusion index, if the response is 20% "Better," 70% "Same," and 10% "Worse," the diffusion index would be 55% (20% + [0.50 x 70%]). A reading of 50% indicates "no change" from the previous month.

Economists and statisticians have determined that the farther the index is away from the amount that would indicate "no change" (50%), the rate of change is greater. Therefore, an index of 60% indicates a faster rate of increase than an index of 55% (increased activity is becoming more dispersed), and an index of 35% indicates a faster rate of decrease than an index of 40% (decreased activity is becoming more dispersed). A value of 100 indicates all respondents are reporting increased activity, and 0 indicates that all respondents report decreased activity. See http://www.ism.ws/ISMReport/content.cfm?ItemNumber=10706.

manufacturing sector of the economy compared with the prior month. A reading less than 50 represents contraction, and a reading of 50 indicates an equal balance between manufacturers reporting advances and declines in their business. **Figure 17** shows the relationship between the ISM Manufacturing PMI and monthly new orders for industrial machinery as reported by the U.S. Census Bureau.

Although the ISM Manufacturing Indexes are among some of the timeliest economic indicators that can be used to gauge the overall health of the industrial machinery segment, it is also difficult to accurately generalize about such a diverse group of companies. For example, other more narrowly defined indicators—such as energy exploration and production activity, highway spending, and certain regulatory changes—could be much more relevant indicators of demand for some of the companies in the industrial machinery segment than the broader economic indicators previously discussed. Given the diverse nature of the industry, the primary drivers of demand will vary according to the different end market(s) served by each particular company.

Figure 17.

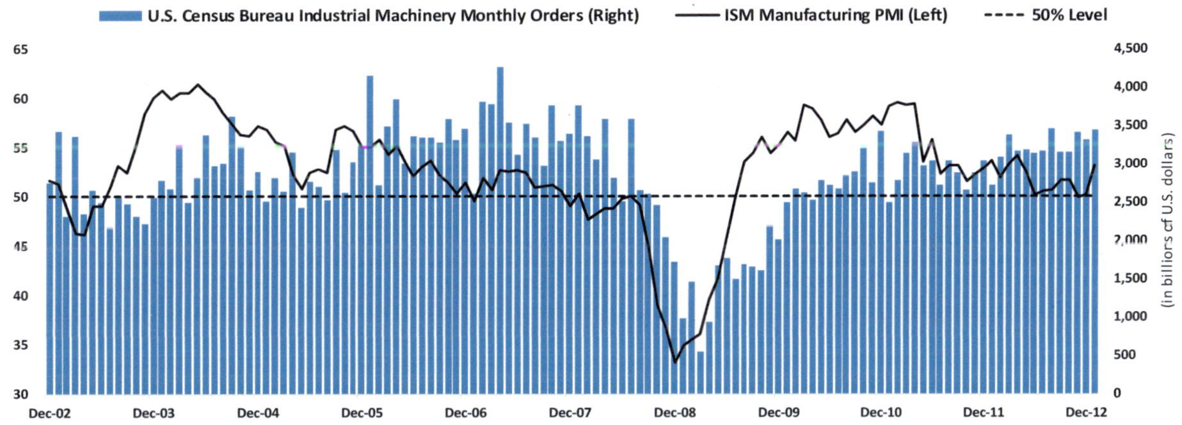

Sources: U.S. Census Bureau; Institute for Supply Management.

COMPETITIVE ANALYSIS

As previously discussed, the construction and mining equipment, farm machinery, and heavy truck segments of the machinery industry are highly consolidated markets, with a handful of OEMs accounting for the vast majority of global industry sales. The competitive environment in each of these segments is characterized by a small number of global competitors and a larger number of regional and local manufacturers of differing strengths. Heavy machinery companies primarily compete on the basis of price, features, quality, service, and anticipated resale value. In developed markets of the world, buyers of heavy machinery will often place greater emphasis on features, including performance and productivity features that can lower the total cost of ownership, whereas buyers of machinery in developing economies tend to be more sensitive to the initial purchase price. Irrespective of the market or region of the world, the strength of the OEM's dealer network is a key determinant of a company's overall competitiveness.

The dealer network often plays a vital role in determining the level of success a machinery company will ultimately realize. When differences in price, features, and perceived quality are small, the strength of the dealer network provides a key point of differentiation that can influence the customer's purchase decision. Some of the ways that dealers are able to distinguish themselves from one another include proximity to the customer, breadth of inventory, availability of replacement parts, and the ability to service and repair the equipment sold. Moreover, relationships between customers and dealers, once established, often persist for long periods of time because the dealer can become a trusted adviser to the customer. Caterpillar, for example, claims that many of its independent dealers have relationships with their customers that span multiple generations.

Well-established dealer networks can also act as a barrier to entry to potential new entrants to the market. It would take a new entrant many years to build a distribution network of its own, and the up-front costs would likely be prohibitive in many cases. An example of just how effective an established dealer network can be at staving off potential competitors is Caterpillar's global dealer network, which the company acknowledges is one of its most important competitive advantages.

Caterpillar's global dealer network is the most extensive distribution network for construction and mining equipment in the world. As of 2012, the company's dealer network consisted of 189 dealers, serving 182 countries and operating 3,494 places of business. By maintaining such an extensive dealer network, Caterpillar is generally able to charge higher prices for its equipment than its competitors are. This is because in addition to purchase price, maintenance expense and uptime contribute significantly to the total cost of ownership. Therefore, proximity to a dealer with strong aftermarket service and in-stock parts availability can lower the total cost of ownership, enabling Caterpillar to charge higher prices, on average, for its machines.

NOTABLE TRENDS

The machinery industry is a relatively mature industry and one in which replacement demand accounts for an estimated 75% of normalized unit volumes in most developed markets. Although almost all machinery wears out over time, a customer often has a significant amount of discretion over the timing of replacement and, in some cases, can defer the purchase of a new machine for several years or more. This ability to defer replacement is another primary factor responsible for the above average cyclicality that characterizes the machinery industry.

Despite the mature, replacement-driven demand environment, several trends happening within the machinery industry are worth discussing. After spending much of the past decade designing equipment that would comply with increasingly stringent governmental emission requirements, heavy truck manufacturers are now placing a greater focus on improving the fuel economy of their vehicles. In construction machinery, a growing equipment rental market has created both benefits and potential risks for OEMs. Last, but not least, after several decades of offshoring production, the competitiveness of the U.S. manufacturing sector appears to be on the rise.

IMPROVING THE FUEL ECONOMY OF HEAVY TRUCKS

A typical heavy duty truck in North America is driven roughly 100,000 miles, on average, per annum. Assuming a price per gallon of diesel of USD4.00 and average fuel economy for a Class 8 truck of approximately 6 mpg, the annual fuel expenditures are around USD67 thousand, or about half the estimated purchase price of a new vehicle.[3] Given the significance of fuel costs, improvements in fuel economy can result in increased profitability for the owner/lessee of a truck and generate a compelling return on the purchase/lease of a new and more fuel-efficient truck. Consider, for example, the impact that a 2 mpg increase in fuel economy could have on annual fuel costs and the corresponding return on a new truck investment. Again, assuming USD4.00 per gallon diesel and 100,000 truck miles per year, a 2 mpg increase in fuel economy would generate annual fuel savings of around 4,200 gallons per year, or close to a USD17 thousand reduction in annual fuel cost (see **Table 3**). Moreover, if we include the estimated savings from such items

[3]The author estimates that the average price of a Class 8 truck in the United States was about USD130,000 in 2012.

as lower maintenance costs associated with a new vehicle and the corresponding opportunity cost of taking a vehicle out of service while maintenance work is performed, the total annual operating cost savings is likely to be in the range of USD22 thousand to USD25 thousand, an attractive return on investment.

Table 3. Impact of Improved Fuel Economy on Fuel Costs

	Fuel Economy (mpg)		
Factors	**6**	**8**	**Est. Savings**
Miles Driven Annually	100,000	100,000	
Fuel Consumption (gallons)	16,667	12,500	4,167
Price of Diesel (per gallon)	$4.00	$4.00	
Annual Fuel Cost	$66,667	$50,000	$16,667

Future improvements in the fuel economy of heavy trucks are likely to come from advancements in engine and transmission technologies as well as from more coordinated integration of the two in order to optimize efficiency. Some of the major OEMs, including Freightliner (a division of Daimler) and Volvo, have already begun integrating their engines and transmissions. Component suppliers Cummins (engines) and Eaton (transmissions) recently announced an integrated powertrain package that is expected to deliver a 3–6% improvement in fuel economy and also lower preventative maintenance costs. Additionally, Eaton and Navistar (engines) also recently announced an integrated drivetrain product that is expected to deliver fuel economy improvements of between 2% and 4%.

Finally, it should be mentioned that another significant factor, apart from the benefits of improved fuel economy, that is helping to drive greater vertical integration within the industry is a desire by the OEMs to increase the size of their aftermarket parts and service operations, which are often the most profitable and least cyclical part of their business.

GROWING IMPORTANCE OF THE RENTAL CHANNEL IN NORTH AMERICA

The construction equipment rental industry in North America has been growing at a faster pace than the overall market for construction machinery for the past couple decades, as evidenced by an approximate 10-fold increase in the rental penetration rate from around 5% in 1993 to roughly half the market in 2012.[4]

[4]It should be noted that the rental fleet population is heavily skewed toward aerial work platforms (AWP) and reach forks, which together represent an estimated 60% of industry rental units. Earthmoving equipment represents approximately 15% of rental units.

Several of the more compelling arguments in favor of renting equipment relate to capital requirements, business uncertainty, flexibility, and cost savings. First, capital requirements: Renting eliminates the need for a large capital investment and lowers the required investment in working capital because equipment inventory needs are minimized. Second, business uncertainty: Equipment users are more likely to rent than purchase during times of significant economic or business uncertainty. Third, flexibility: Renting provides end-users increased flexibility to more easily manage their changing equipment requirements. Fourth, cost savings: Renting reduces certain costs related to equipment storage and disposal.

Growth in the rental channel has both positive and negative implications for the traditional OEM/dealer business model. Potential benefits include increased market penetration and improved profitability, with the risk being the diminution of a primary barrier to entry and source of competitive advantage vis-à-vis brand and dealer relevance.

By making equipment more accessible and reducing the risks associated with owning, an active rental channel can increase the market penetration of construction equipment in both strong economic times (in order to accommodate peak periods of demand) and in a weak economic environment (when business is slow and uncertainty is high). Moreover, the rental channel also has the potential to improve OEM and/or dealer profitability because of an increase in the available supply of used machines. Most rental companies maintain a relatively young fleet of equipment (the typical age of equipment is 30–40 months). Consequently, the rental channel tends to generate a steady supply of relatively well-maintained and low-hour-used machines for dealers to sell. Because used machines are more profitable for the dealer to sell than new machines, dealer profitability is enhanced. Moreover, an increase in the used equipment population is the primary driver of demand for higher margin parts and service revenue, which benefit both the OEM and dealer.

In addition to the benefits, the non-OEM-controlled portion of the rental channel also presents some potential risks to the already established OEMs. In a rental transaction, for example, a customer is typically more focused on the rental company's level of service than with things such as brand of machine, dealer network, warranty program, or resale value—all of which are competitive points of differentiation among OEMs and are important factors that weigh heavily in any purchase decision. Consequently, from an end-user perspective, a significant portion of an OEM's competitive advantage is potentially marginalized in a rental transaction.

A growing rental channel also has the potential to diminish the strength of an OEM's dealer network, one of the industry's most important barriers to entry. As previously discussed, a strong dealer network is vital to the long-term success of the OEM, and the cost of establishing a network of dealers is by far the industry's largest barrier to entry. Manufacturers wishing to enter the North American market also face a number of other challenges, including an unfamiliar brand and the lack of an existing installed base of machines. The importance of an existing installed base of machines should not be overlooked because that is what drives demand for parts and services, the sales of which are necessary in order for a dealer to achieve profitability. That said, one or more of the national rental companies, which are not controlled by the OEMs, could potentially provide manufacturers looking to enter the North American market with an avenue of opportunity. If, for example, an overseas manufacturer were able to successfully negotiate an agreement (sales, partnership, acquisition, etc.) with one of the national rental companies, it could potentially have a direct path to market and an opportunity to build its presence in North America.

It's not clear at this stage what the net impact on sales and profitability will ultimately be on the existing OEMs; Caterpillar, Komatsu, Volvo, Deere, and CNH Global currently control an estimated 85% of the U.S. construction equipment market. For now, the OEMs appear to be pursuing a multi-pronged approach to channel distribution, including a mix of independent and company-owned dealers, national and private rental companies, and OEM direct sales. Caterpillar, for example, has almost doubled the number of CAT-branded rental stores from 650 in 2000 to 1,249 in 2012, representing just over a third of the total number of CAT stores.

U.S. MANUFACTURING RENAISSANCE

The United States is increasingly being viewed by a growing number of companies as an attractive location to manufacture products destined for North America. The erosion of China's manufacturing cost advantage has accelerated in recent years, mostly because of rapidly rising labor costs in China and relatively low energy prices in the United States.

According to the National Bureau of Statistics of China, labor costs in China over the 10-year period from 2001 to 2011 (most recent available) increased at a compound annual growth rate of 16%, resulting in a quadrupling of wages over the same time period. Over the past five years, wage growth has accelerated to 18% per annum, led by a 32% jump in 2011 alone. Recent labor unrest in China has contributed to the dramatic increase in wages. For example, Foxconn Technology Group—a subsidiary of Hon Hai Precision Industry Company and the world's largest contract manufacturer of electronics—more than doubled wages for its Shenzhen factory employees in 2010 following a number of worker suicides earlier that year.[5] **Figure 18** illustrates the rapid growth in Chinese wages over the past several decades.

[5]See http://www.bloomberg.com/news/2010-06-06/foxconn-to-double-china-factory-worker-salaries-by-october-after-suicides.html.

Figure 18. Average Annual Wage of Employee in China

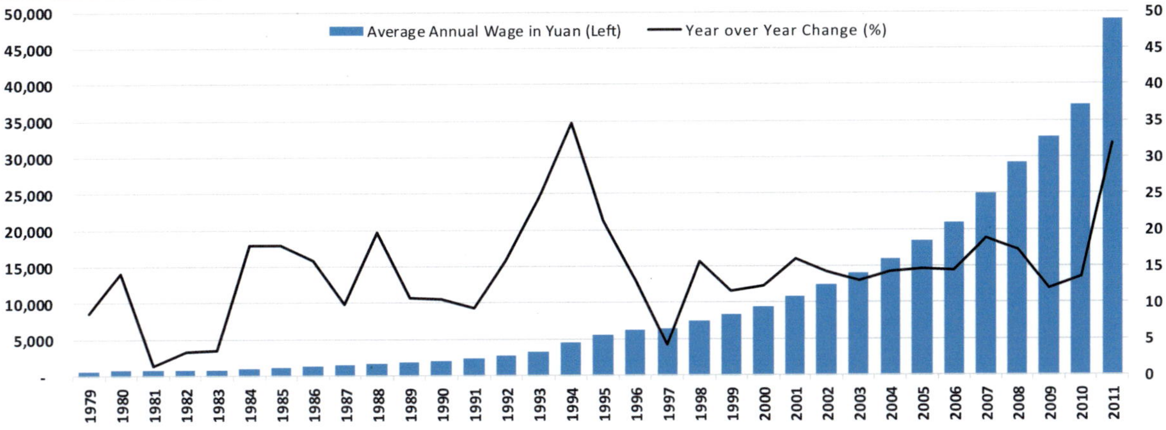

Source: National Bureau of Statistics in China.

Apart from labor costs, declining U.S. energy prices are also helping to boost the competitiveness of manufacturers in the United States. Technological advances in horizontal drilling and hydraulic fracturing methods have driven dramatic growth in U.S. shale gas production in recent years. The result has been declining natural gas prices, where the average price in 2012 was less than half the average price just five years earlier. The United States now has among the lowest natural gas prices in the world (see **Figure 19**).

Low natural gas prices are particularly beneficial to chemical companies because natural gas is the fuel that powers most chemical and refining processes. More than a dozen chemical makers have already announced plans or have begun expanding operations in the United States to take advantage of low natural gas prices.[6]

[6]See http://www.bloomberg.com/news/2012-01-18/shale-gas-boom-spurs-methanex-to-relocate-idled-chilean-plant-to-louisiana.html.

Figure 19. Average Yearly Price of U.S. Natural Gas (NYM $/btu)

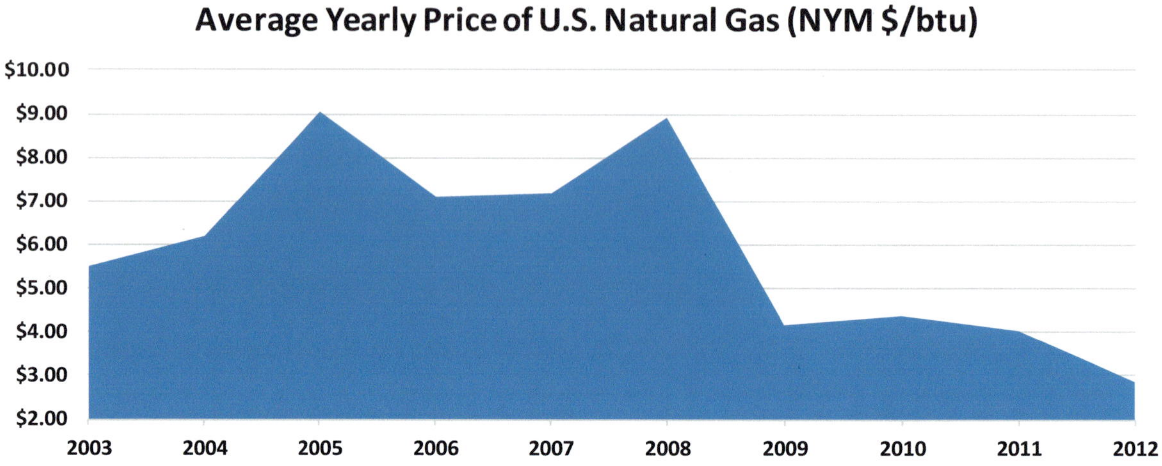

Note: As quoted in USD per British thermal unit on the New York Mercantile Exchange.

Source: FactSet.

FINANCIAL STATEMENT ANALYSIS

REVENUE

All revenue is not created equal. A key to understanding the strength or weakness of a machinery company's top line is to analyze the underlying drivers of the change in terms of unit volumes, pricing, currency, and acquisitions or divestitures. In terms of disclosure, some companies are better about including this optional information in their regulatory filings than others. A rich resource for this level of granularity is the company's earnings conference calls. All else being equal, organic growth (volume and price) is much more telling about the underlying business of a company than total revenue growth because the latter may be distorted by changes in foreign exchange (FX) and acquisition activity. When possible, always try to isolate and track the organic changes in revenue for a company. If management doesn't readily disclose this information, then ask for it in a public forum.

When companies do not disclose organic growth statistics, they are still frequently possible to estimate. For example, if a company discloses that a recent acquisition contributed USD30 million of sales during the period and beginning-of-period sales were USD1 billion, we can estimate that acquisition activity contributed 3% to total revenue growth during the period. If total reported revenue growth during the period was 8%, and assuming no impact from currency movement, estimated organic revenue growth during the period would be 5% (total revenue growth of 8% less inorganic growth through acquisition of 3% equals 5% organic growth). Organic revenue growth provides a much better basis than total revenue growth from which to compare a company's growth over time versus its peers or the industry. Moreover, comparative analysis based on organic sales growth can often yield important insights into pricing strategies and shifts in market share among companies. However, it should be noted that organic sales growth is rarely a pure apples-to-apples comparison; changes in the sales mix and differences in the composition of products sold among competing companies often make for an imperfect comparison.

Most machinery companies recognize substantially all of the revenue from a sale when the product is shipped to a dealer or customer or when a service is rendered. Two exceptions to this practice occur (1) under long-term contracts, where revenue may be recognized on a percentage-of-completion basis, and (2) in sales that are subject to a residual value guarantee.

Revenue from the sale of large turbines, certain mining equipment (including draglines, large shovels, and roof support systems), and other machinery that requires a relatively long time to manufacture is frequently recognized using the percentage-of-completion method. Under this approach, a company will recognize a portion of the total revenue from a long-term sales contract based on the ratio of actual costs incurred to total estimated costs to be incurred. This method of revenue recognition relies on certain estimates provided by management, which are subject to adjustment over the course of manufacture.

Sales that are subject to residual value guarantees (RVGs) are common in the heavy truck segment of the machinery industry. RVGs are used by many of the OEMs in the heavy truck market as a way to incentivize buyers to purchase their equipment. The guarantees are commonly offered based on either a trade-in or buy-back value. In a trade-in, the buyer will receive a credit toward the purchase of a new truck. In the more aggressive buy-back, the buyer essentially has a put option on the equipment because the seller is obligated to repurchase the equipment at the "guaranteed" price. When equipment is sold subject to an RVG, the full sales price is received from the customer. From an accounting perspective, a liability is established for the residual value obligation with the remainder of the proceeds recorded as deferred lease revenue. The deferred lease revenue is then typically amortized on a straight-line basis over the RVG contract period.

GROSS MARGIN

A key indicator of profitability, gross margin as a percentage of sales reflects both the pricing power of a business and the efficiency of the machinery company's manufacturing operations. Generally, companies with relatively low production costs, a high percentage of revenue from aftermarket sales, and/or pricing power will have higher gross margins than those of its peers. For example, Nordson Corporation, a manufacturer of specialty adhesive dispensing products and systems for industrial applications, consistently earns among the highest gross margins in the machinery sector, averaging 58% over the past five years, nearly double the median gross margin of 30% for the machinery industry. Nordson's high gross margins reflect a combination of (1) its market-leading positions in a variety of niche end markets (greater than 50% market share in some cases), which provide the company with certain scale advantages; (2) a high percentage of recurring revenue from aftermarket parts and consumables, which have represented ~40–45% of total revenue on average (as a rule of thumb, most aftermarket sales carry higher-than-corporate-average margins); and (3) limited competition in its niche markets, which has provided the company with a certain degree of pricing power.

Gross margin percentage is the most stable of the various profit margin metrics because of the high percentage of variable costs that make up cost of goods sold. Variability in gross margin usually results from a variety of sources.

1. *Changes in raw material prices and other input costs.* Although many machinery companies are able to pass through changes in input costs to their customers, it is often accomplished with a lag of one to two quarters.[7] Thus, fluctuations in input costs can create short-term variability in otherwise relatively stable gross margins.
2. *A "mix-shift," or a shift in the proportion of revenue derived from the sale of high margin items versus low margin items.* For example, machinery companies with an aftermarket business will frequently experience a positive lift to gross margins from a mix-shift during periods of weak demand as customers look to defer purchases of new equipment and instead opt to repair and maintain existing equipment, which drives an increased proportion of sales of higher gross margin parts and service business for machinery companies.[8]
3. *The over- or under-absorption of overhead costs.* As an accounting refresher, fixed manufacturing overhead costs (e.g., depreciation, property taxes, and utilities) are usually applied to products sold based on a predetermined overhead rate, which, in turn, is based on management's forecast of production volumes. To the extent that actual production volumes fall short of management's forecast, the fixed overhead rate will be "under-absorbed" because fewer units are produced than expected. As these units are eventually sold from inventory, the higher unit costs will negatively impact gross margins. Conversely, and all else being equal, gross margins will benefit from an over-absorption of costs because a fixed overhead rate is applied to more units of production than expected, resulting in lower unit costs.
4. *Changes in net pricing.* When a company is able to raise prices net of any increase in its input costs, it is said to have pricing power. Besides the positive impact it can have on gross margin, companies with pricing power also have another way of preserving or improving profitability during a sluggish economic environment.

[7]It should be noted that the ability of companies to raise prices in response to changes in input costs is not uniform across the machinery sector. Some companies may be locked into long-term pricing agreements with their customers that limit how often and by how much a company can raise its prices during a particular time frame. Other machinery companies may be able to respond much more quickly to rising raw material prices and then hang on to the raised prices for an extended period of time even as input costs decline.

[8]However, this positive effect may not be enough to overcome the negative impact of under-absorption caused by lower-than-planned production volumes.

5. *Changes in productivity.* Management of machinery companies frequently implement a number of initiatives to improve the efficiency of the company's manufacturing operations. Common initiatives and programs include lean, six sigma, supply chain management, and various enterprise resource planning systems. The impact on gross margins from the benefits associated with various productivity-improvement initiatives tends to be longer term in nature than those previously discussed, with most of the impact on gross margin appearing more gradually over time.

RAW MATERIAL COSTS

Many machinery companies—including manufacturers of construction, mining, and agricultural equipment and makers of heavy trucks—are significant users of steel, copper, and other metals for the manufacture of their products. Unanticipated increases in the prices of such commodities can have a significant impact on a company's costs and negatively impact profitability to the extent that the company is unable to fully offset the effect of the increased costs through price increases, productivity improvements, or cost-reduction programs. Manufacturers will typically seek to manage this commodity price risk through the purchase and/or sale of commodity forward and option contracts.

OPERATING MARGIN

Operating margin is a more comprehensive measure of profitability than gross margin because it indicates how much money a company makes from the actual operations of its business before the effects of financing and taxes. Although the absolute level of the operating margin is telling about the profitability of a company's operations (higher being better, with 10% representing the average operating margin for a machinery company), analysts should also pay close attention to changes in the operating margin.[9]

The direction and magnitude of changes in the operating margin, especially in relation to changes in sales, bear careful monitoring. A particularly useful metric in this regard is the incremental operating margin, which measures how much operating profit is generated from each additional dollar of revenue. Mathematically, the

[9]The use of averages to describe something does not always provide adequate perspective about the degree of variability around the mean, and that is especially applicable in the case of an *average* operating margin. As Ohio State football coach Woody Hayes once said, "Statistics always remind me of the fellow who drowned in a river whose average depth was three feet."

ratio is calculated as the change in operating income divided by the change in revenues, with the result expressed as a percentage that is comparable with operating margins. The average incremental operating margin[10] of a machinery company is about 30%, based on a median normalized operating margin of 10% and assuming an average fixed cost structure of 20–25%. A 30% incremental margin implies that each additional dollar of revenue will contribute USD0.30 to operating income, which is also a useful way of describing the amount of operating leverage in the business. As revenues increase, a primary objective for management is to drive margin expansion by leveraging both the fixed cost component of selling, general, and administrative expenses (SG&A) and the indirect fixed costs in cost of goods sold (COGS). Incremental operating margins are a useful scorecard to measure the effectiveness of management in this regard.

Although companies with relatively high incremental operating margins will experience a more rapid expansion of operating profits during an up cycle, companies with high operating leverage will experience a more rapid decline of operating profits during a down cycle. Moreover, the average incremental operating margin experienced during an up cycle will usually be significantly less than the decremental operating margins generated during the early stages of a down cycle because sales initially fall much faster than the company is able to cut costs.[11] Thus, operating leverage for cyclical companies is a double-edged sword; management must weigh the tradeoff between higher peak margins during the up cycle versus earnings protection during the down cycle.

Incremental margins, although a key indicator of profitability, are one of the most volatile operating metrics that machinery analysts track. For the ratio to be meaningful, both revenue and operating profits need to be moving in the same direction because dividing an increase (decrease) in revenue by a decrease (increase) in operating income would result in a negative number. Moreover, as the change in revenue approaches zero, the incremental margin approaches infinity. Finally, currency translation can distort the incremental operating margins of machinery companies with multinational operations.

Tables 4a and **4b** illustrate the distribution of normalized gross and operating margins for the entire universe of U.S. machinery companies that were examined in this report.

[10]See footnote 9.

[11]The term **decremental operating margin** is used in place of incremental operating margin when both revenue and operating income are declining. The same formula is used to calculate both ratios, with decremental operating margin measuring the decline in operating income for each additional dollar of revenue that is lost.

Table 4a. U.S. Machinery Industry Distribution of Gross Margins (10-year median values)

Gross Margin	# of Companies	% of Total
10–20%	8	11%
20–30%	28	40%
30–40%	26	37%
40–50%	6	9%
50–60%	2	3%
Median = 30%	70	100%

Table 4b. U.S. Machinery Industry Distribution of Operating Margins (10-year median values)

Operating Margin	# of Companies	% of Total
1–5%	6	9%
5–10%	26	37%
10–15%	30	43%
15–20%	7	10%
20–25%	1	1%
Median = 10%	70	100%

FINANCIAL SUBSIDIARIES

Another nuance to keep in mind when analyzing the financial statements of machinery companies is the use of financial subsidiaries. Some of the larger manufacturers of heavy machinery—including Caterpillar, Deere, PACCAR, CNH Global, and Navistar—operate wholly owned financial subsidiaries to help facilitate the sale and/or lease of their products. A significant portion of a machinery company's earnings may be derived from the income generated by its financial subsidiary, especially during cyclical downturns in the industry. Consequently, it is important to consider some of the risks associated with these operations as well as their potential impact on consolidated earnings.

The two primary risk factors associated with these types of financial subsidiaries are credit default risk and residual value risk. The credit default risk arises from the fact that not all of the borrowers who finance the purchase or lease of equipment will make their obligated payments. Companies can manage this risk by adhering to disciplined underwriting standards during the origination of the loan and lease agreements. Residual value risk, as previously discussed in the section related to revenue, is the risk that the market value of the equipment at the end of the contract will be less than what the finance company estimated at the time of origination. In the late 1990s, certain heavy truck manufacturers offered unusually high RVGs in an attempt to capture market share. This contributed to a glut of used commercial vehicle inventory several years later, which depressed prices and resulted in significant write-downs at the finance companies, which, in turn, were forced to pay above-market prices for used trucks. Although the heavy truck industry has subsequently pared back its aggressive use of RVGs, analysts should be aware of this potential risk when investigating a machinery company with a financial subsidiary.

Apart from the potential risks, analysts should also be aware that a significant portion of a machinery company's earnings may be derived from the income generated by its financial subsidiary, especially during cyclical downturns in the industry. As **Table 5** shows, a machinery company's financial subsidiary becomes an increasingly important source of earnings during periods of weak industry demand.

Table 5. Finance Subsidiary Net Income as % of Total Net Income

Company	Fiscal	2003	2004	2005	2006	2007	2008	2009	2010	2011	2012
Caterpillar	Dec	24%	17%	14%	14%	14%	13%	23%	13%	9%	10%
Deere & Co.	Oct	51%	22%	24%	23%	20%	16%	17%	19%	17%	15%
PACCAR	Dec	15%	12%	11%	11%	16%	15%	53%	23%	16%	19%
CNH Global	Dec	100%	82%	89%	61%	37%	29%	NM	32%	24%	26%
Navistar	Oct	NM	NM	94%	37%	NM	NM	17%	40%	28%	NM

Note: NM = not meaningful.

Sources: Company reports; author estimates.

LEVERAGE

A typical machinery company will target a long-term debt-to-capital structure between 25% and 35% and/or or a leverage ratio of about 1.5 times debt-to-EBITDA (earnings before interest, taxes, depreciation, and amortization). Again, there is significant variation around these averages: Some companies within the machinery group have maintained a debt-free balance sheet throughout much of their history, whereas others have levered up to 4 times EBITDA or more for short periods of time to consummate an acquisition.

PENSION AND OTHER POST-EMPLOYMENT BENEFITS (OPEB)

Although not unique to the machinery sector of the market, employee retirement plan obligations are a significant burden for most machinery companies. In this study, 54 out of the 70 machinery companies in our universe had defined benefit pension plans, of which all but one were underfunded as of December 2012 (with underfunding equal to 8% of market capitalization, on average). Despite strong returns on retirement plan assets over the past several years, plan deficits have increased because of a decline in discount rates, which has driven up the projected benefit obligations of the plans. At the end of 2012, the average machinery company's pension plan was 70% funded. In terms of the income statement, net pension expense for machinery companies was equal to 5% of operating income, on average, in 2012.

OTHER

Many of the other important aspects of financial statement analysis for machinery companies—including the analysis of working capital, free cash flow conversion, and returns on invested capital—are similar to those applied in other industries. However, given the cyclicality of the machinery industry, one should view all financial metrics within the context of an entire cycle (including peak and trough periods) in an effort to identify the "mid-cycle" characteristics of the company. **Table 6** shows historical valuation and operating statistics (10-year median values) for machinery companies.

Table 6. Historical Valuation & Operating Statistics (10-year median values)

		EV/SALES		EV/EBITDA		P/E		LTM Margins				Div	Payout		Net Debt (Cash)/EBITDA		Working Capital % of Sales			
Ticker	Company	LTM	NTM	LTM	NTM	LTM	NTM	Gross	EBIT	EBITDA	Net Inc	Yield	Ratio	LTM RoIC		Capital	AR	INV	AP	NWC
AGCO	AGCO Corp.	0.6	0.5	8.0	6.2	14.4	12.7	17.4%	5.9%	7.5%	3.2%	0.0%	0%	12.0%	0.6	14%	12%	18%	11%	19%
AIMC	Altra Holdings Inc.	1.1	1.0	7.4	6.6	17.4	13.1	27.7%	10.2%	14.0%	4.4%	0.0%	0%	14.6%	2.3	60%	12%	15%	7%	21%
AIN	Albany International Corp.	1.3	1.2	7.3	7.1	16.6	16.1	39.0%	9.4%	15.9%	5.8%	1.3%	38%	6.7%	1.5	35%	19%	20%	5%	32%
AIT	Applied Industrial Technologies	0.6	0.5	8.7	7.3	17.7	14.2	27.0%	5.9%	7.0%	3.6%	1.9%	32%	18.6%	(0.2)	–8%	12%	10%	5%	17%
ALG	Alamo Group Inc.	0.5	0.5	7.6	6.4	15.6	12.6	21.4%	5.5%	7.1%	3.3%	1.1%	17%	8.0%	0.9	12%	22%	21%	7%	35%
ASTE	Astec Industries Inc.	0.8	0.7	10.4	8.3	18.8	18.1	23.0%	6.3%	8.5%	4.1%	0.0%	0%	8.1%	(0.4)	–9%	9%	27%	6%	30%
ATU	Actuant Corp.	1.7	1.5	10.4	9.2	18.9	15.2	33.2%	12.9%	15.5%	7.6%	0.1%	3%	25.7%	1.9	48%	13%	13%	10%	16%
B	Barnes Group Inc.	1.2	1.1	9.8	8.3	16.2	14.2	35.6%	8.5%	12.4%	5.3%	2.3%	34%	10.1%	2.1	39%	14%	17%	9%	20%
BGG	Briggs & Stratton Corp.	0.6	0.7	7.2	6.7	16.8	16.6	18.8%	4.8%	7.9%	2.9%	2.5%	66%	6.6%	1.1	23%	13%	21%	7%	25%
BLT	Blount International Inc.	1.4	1.3	7.6	8.1	14.3	15.0	33.0%	14.6%	18.7%	6.2%	0.0%	0%	22.9%	2.9	132%	13%	14%	5%	21%
CAT	Caterpillar Inc.	1.2	1.1	10.0	7.9	14.4	12.0	22.1%	10.0%	13.2%	7.8%	1.8%	27%	19.8%	0.8	32%	10%	16%	11%	17%
CFX	Colfax Corp	1.5	0.9	8.3	5.9	20.1	16.9	35.0%	12.8%	15.7%	5.3%	0.0%	0%	9.5%	1.2	38%	15%	12%	8%	19%
CIR	Circor International Inc.	0.9	0.8	7.9	7.2	17.6	15.6	29.3%	7.7%	10.2%	5.0%	0.5%	10%	10.8%	(0.1)	–1%	17%	24%	10%	31%
CLC	CLARCOR Inc.	1.8	1.7	11.0	9.9	20.5	18.6	30.7%	14.0%	16.7%	9.1%	0.9%	19%	19.2%	(0.1)	–4%	17%	14%	6%	26%
CMCO	Columbus McKinnon Corp.	0.7	0.7	7.8	7.2	12.3	11.6	26.6%	7.9%	10.5%	4.4%	0.0%	0%	13.8%	1.9	31%	16%	16%	6%	24%
CMI	Cummins Inc.	0.7	0.7	7.2	5.8	13.8	9.8	21.6%	8.7%	11.4%	5.6%	1.3%	13%	17.1%	0.0	0%	14%	12%	9%	17%
CNH	CNH Global N.V.	0.4	0.4	5.9	4.8	16.4	15.5	17.9%	6.4%	8.5%	3.2%	0.6%	14%	5.7%	(0.0)	–1%	9%	22%	16%	16%
CR	Crane Co.	1.0	1.0	8.4	7.6	14.5	12.6	33.0%	10.3%	13.2%	6.9%	1.7%	28%	13.8%	0.6	16%	13%	14%	7%	20%
DCI	Donaldson Co. Inc.	1.8	1.7	13.2	12.1	22.9	20.3	32.6%	11.0%	13.7%	7.8%	0.9%	22%	17.9%	0.4	15%	18%	10%	9%	19%
DE	Deere & Co.	1.1	0.9	10.1	7.6	15.8	13.1	23.6%	9.6%	11.6%	8.0%	1.7%	25%	13.7%	(0.2)	–9%	14%	11%	7%	19%
DOV	Dover Corp.	1.6	1.5	9.2	8.9	16.6	14.5	36.1%	13.9%	17.1%	9.1%	1.7%	27%	21.4%	1.1	23%	15%	10%	6%	20%
ESE	ESCO Technologies Inc.	1.8	1.7	10.6	11.0	20.6	21.5	36.5%	12.4%	16.3%	7.6%	0.0%	0%	12.7%	0.3	3%	18%	12%	8%	21%
ETN	Eaton Corporation PLC	1.2	1.0	9.6	7.9	13.8	12.1	28.1%	9.2%	13.0%	7.3%	2.1%	32%	13.1%	1.4	33%	15%	10%	8%	17%
FLS	Flowserve Corp.	1.2	1.0	8.7	7.9	15.9	13.9	33.0%	12.2%	14.2%	8.0%	0.5%	11%	23.9%	0.6	19%	16%	17%	12%	22%
FSS	Federal Signal Corp.	0.8	0.7	12.1	8.4	20.5	15.5	25.0%	5.0%	7.4%	2.4%	2.6%	47%	7.4%	3.8	41%	15%	15%	7%	24%
GDI	Gardner Denver Inc.	1.3	1.2	8.7	6.8	16.6	11.2	31.8%	13.9%	16.6%	8.6%	0.0%	0%	18.5%	1.1	22%	18%	14%	7%	24%

(continued)

Table 6. Historical Valuation & Operating Statistics (10-year median values) (continued)

		EV/SALES		EV/EBITDA		P/E		LTM Margins				Div	Payout		Net Debt (Cash)/EBITDA		Working Capital % of Sales			
Ticker	Company	LTM	NTM	LTM	NTM	LTM	NTM	Gross	EBIT	EBITDA	Net Inc	Yield	Ratio	LTM RoIC		Capital	AR	INV	AP	NWC
GGG	Graco Inc.	3.2	3.0	11.9	10.5	20.8	18.2	53.2%	24.3%	28.0%	16.0%	1.8%	38%	43.2%	0.2	12%	16%	10%	3%	22%
GHM	Graham Corp.	1.2	0.9	10.5	8.0	24.0	16.1	29.2%	11.6%	13.4%	6.9%	0.5%	9%	24.7%	(3.1)	−119%	24%	9%	8%	25%
GTLS	Chart Industries Inc.	1.4	1.2	8.6	7.0	16.6	14.5	29.9%	12.2%	15.6%	6.8%	0.0%	0%	15.3%	1.2	34%	18%	14%	8%	24%
HDNG	Hardinge Inc.	0.5	0.6	7.2	5.0	10.7	9.3	32.8%	5.4%	8.4%	2.0%	0.5%	10%	4.5%	1.3	11%	21%	40%	9%	52%
HURC	Hurco Cos.	0.7	0.7	6.5	4.8	10.7	9.5	31.1%	10.3%	12.5%	7.0%	0.0%	0%	15.7%	(0.6)	−40%	15%	34%	16%	33%
IEX	IDEX Corp.	2.2	2.0	10.7	9.4	19.3	16.6	41.0%	17.5%	20.9%	10.9%	1.4%	28%	26.4%	1.1	23%	13%	12%	6%	19%
IR	Ingersoll-Rand Plc	1.2	1.2	9.9	8.7	15.0	12.8	27.4%	10.7%	13.2%	7.4%	1.3%	21%	13.9%	1.1	23%	16%	11%	8%	19%
ITT	ITT Corp	1.3	1.1	9.8	8.0	18.1	14.6	28.6%	10.7%	13.3%	1.1%	1.0%	16%	20.4%	0.5	19%	15%	9%	11%	13%
ITW	Illinois Tool Works Inc.	1.9	1.8	10.0	9.1	16.8	15.1	34.9%	16.1%	19.3%	10.6%	2.1%	33%	21.2%	0.5	14%	16%	10%	5%	21%
JBT	John Bean Technologies Corp.	0.6	0.6	6.6	6.3	13.9	11.8	24.8%	6.6%	9.2%	3.9%	1.5%	22%	15.4%	1.0	57%	18%	12%	8%	22%
JOY	Joy Global Inc.	1.7	1.4	11.8	7.0	20.5	14.4	31.7%	18.4%	20.3%	12.2%	0.9%	19%	26.5%	0.3	15%	17%	25%	8%	34%
KAI	Kadant Inc.	1.0	0.9	9.0	8.3	20.4	15.9	40.1%	9.2%	11.7%	6.7%	0.0%	0%	16.2%	(0.9)	−19%	16%	14%	9%	22%
KAMN	Kaman Corp.	0.6	0.5	10.2	8.8	17.7	15.2	26.9%	4.8%	6.4%	2.8%	2.2%	41%	8.5%	0.9	16%	14%	20%	7%	28%
KDN	Kaydon Corp.	2.5	2.3	10.2	9.0	20.4	20.0	36.3%	19.5%	24.1%	13.5%	1.8%	34%	20.8%	(1.2)	−41%	14%	16%	5%	25%
KMT	Kennametal Inc.	1.1	1.1	9.2	8.1	17.8	14.6	33.8%	10.1%	12.4%	6.1%	1.4%	23%	12.8%	1.2	19%	16%	19%	7%	27%
LDL	Lydall Inc.	0.5	0.6	6.3	6.5	20.2	18.1	20.7%	3.7%	8.8%	2.5%	0.0%	0%	5.0%	(0.1)	−2%	15%	12%	8%	18%
LECO	Lincoln Electric Holdings Inc.	1.1	1.0	9.0	7.6	15.8	13.3	27.3%	10.3%	12.8%	7.5%	1.7%	27%	15.8%	(0.2)	−7%	14%	15%	7%	23%
LNN	Lindsay Corp.	1.5	1.2	14.2	10.4	26.0	23.0	24.5%	9.2%	11.6%	6.3%	0.7%	21%	13.9%	(1.3)	−36%	15%	11%	5%	21%
MDD	Middleby Corp.	2.1	1.7	10.5	8.6	16.8	14.6	39.1%	18.1%	19.9%	10.4%	0.0%	0%	35.6%	1.5	45%	12%	12%	5%	19%
MTSC	MTS Systems Corp.	1.2	1.1	8.2	7.5	18.4	15.4	42.8%	13.8%	16.0%	9.9%	1.5%	25%	36.0%	(1.5)	−87%	26%	11%	5%	32%
MTW	Manitowoc Co.	1.0	0.9	9.3	7.8	22.1	17.2	22.3%	7.1%	10.3%	2.4%	0.6%	14%	11.9%	3.6	60%	10%	16%	13%	13%
NAV	Navistar International Corp.	0.6	0.6	10.3	9.3	10.4	10.6	17.6%	4.0%	6.6%	2.3%	0.0%	0%	5.8%	5.0	120%	21%	11%	15%	18%
NDSN	Nordson Corp.	2.0	1.9	11.1	9.6	18.5	15.6	56.6%	15.9%	19.7%	10.1%	1.4%	25%	28.7%	1.2	30%	19%	10%	5%	25%
NPO	EnPro Industries Inc.	0.8	0.8	6.1	5.7	12.5	10.5	34.1%	7.3%	12.4%	5.1%	0.0%	0%	6.1%	0.8	16%	14%	8%	6%	15%
OSK	Oshkosh Corp.	0.6	0.6	6.9	6.8	14.1	11.9	16.5%	8.1%	9.7%	4.1%	0.4%	7%	25.0%	0.9	29%	10%	12%	7%	16%
PCAR	PACCAR Corp.	1.0	0.9	9.6	9.5	14.6	14.9	14.1%	8.4%	10.0%	7.2%	3.0%	44%	38.3%	(1.7)	−92%	5%	4%	7%	2%
PH	Parker Hannifin Corp.	1.1	1.0	8.9	7.5	16.7	13.1	21.6%	10.7%	13.8%	6.8%	1.3%	21%	15.6%	0.7	21%	15%	12%	7%	20%

(continued)

Table 6. Historical Valuation & Operating Statistics (10-year median values) (continued)

		EV/SALES		EV/EBITDA		P/E		LTM Margins							Net Debt (Cash)/EBITDA		Working Capital % of Sales			
Ticker	Company	LTM	NTM	LTM	NTM	LTM	NTM	Gross	EBIT	EBITDA	Net Inc	Div Yield	Payout Ratio	LTM RoIC		Capital	AR	INV	AP	NWC
PLL	Pall Corp.	2.1	1.9	12.3	11.1	21.1	19.2	48.9%	14.3%	18.7%	9.4%	1.4%	32%	14.3%	0.7	21%	25%	17%	7%	36%
PLOW	Douglas Dynamics Inc.	2.1	2.3	10.0	10.9	18.3	24.3	33.5%	18.1%	22.7%	6.1%	5.9%	122%	10.1%	3.2	49%	17%	13%	2%	28%
PNR	Pentair Ltd.	1.4	1.3	10.4	9.1	17.5	16.3	29.7%	11.0%	14.0%	6.3%	1.8%	32%	17.7%	1.9	32%	16%	13%	8%	20%
SNA	Snap-On Inc.	1.2	1.1	8.8	8.1	17.2	14.3	45.5%	11.0%	13.6%	6.2%	2.6%	42%	13.3%	1.2	24%	20%	13%	6%	27%
SPW	SPX Corp.	0.9	0.9	8.4	9.0	18.6	16.4	28.3%	7.2%	10.1%	4.0%	1.5%	28%	11.6%	1.9	33%	23%	12%	12%	24%
SWK	Stanley Black & Decker Inc.	1.4	1.2	8.8	8.0	14.9	13.8	36.9%	13.3%	15.6%	7.5%	2.4%	41%	18.8%	1.3	29%	16%	13%	10%	18%
SXI	Standex International Corp.	0.7	0.7	7.8	7.9	14.3	13.6	31.6%	6.6%	8.6%	3.7%	3.0%	50%	9.8%	1.8	33%	16%	13%	10%	18%
TEX	Terex Corp.	0.6	0.6	8.2	7.1	15.1	10.0	15.7%	5.8%	6.8%	2.7%	0.0%	0%	9.8%	1.9	34%	14%	24%	13%	24%
TKR	Timken Co.	0.7	0.7	5.6	5.0	13.8	11.7	20.7%	7.8%	12.5%	4.5%	2.0%	25%	8.9%	0.9	25%	13%	18%	10%	23%
TNC	Tennant Co.	0.9	0.8	9.8	8.9	21.0	19.3	42.0%	6.0%	8.8%	4.0%	1.7%	35%	12.3%	(0.2)	–7%	18%	9%	5%	23%
TTC	Toro Co.	1.1	1.0	9.6	8.3	17.8	15.2	34.7%	10.1%	12.5%	6.3%	1.0%	17%	29.2%	0.5	23%	14%	13%	5%	22%
TWI	Titan International Inc.	1.0	0.8	10.0	7.4	25.8	15.1	12.8%	3.9%	10.2%	1.6%	0.1%	5%	4.8%	2.9	42%	11%	17%	5%	24%
VMI	Valmont Industries Inc.	1.2	1.0	8.7	7.2	17.8	15.0	25.9%	9.5%	12.6%	5.8%	0.7%	12%	14.4%	0.8	26%	16%	14%	7%	22%
WAB	Wabtec	1.4	1.3	10.1	8.2	19.1	14.5	25.8%	13.3%	15.3%	8.1%	0.1%	2%	22.6%	0.4	12%	16%	13%	10%	20%
WTS	Watts Water Technologies Inc.	1.1	1.0	7.8	7.7	17.0	16.0	35.4%	10.2%	13.1%	5.6%	1.2%	21%	13.6%	0.8	15%	16%	22%	9%	30%
WWD	Woodward Inc.	1.5	1.4	10.3	8.8	19.4	17.4	28.7%	11.4%	15.8%	7.6%	0.9%	17%	14.0%	0.9	18%	13%	18%	5%	27%
XYL	Xylem Inc.	1.5	1.4	9.2	8.7	13.8	13.8	37.9%	11.7%	15.5%	9.0%	0.8%	11%	16.9%	0.0	14%	19%	11%	8%	21%
Average		**1.0**	**0.9**	**8.8**	**7.7**	**16.7**	**14.4**	**30.2%**	**10.3%**	**13.3%**	**6.3%**	**1.1%**	**20%**	**16.2%**	**0.8**	**16%**	**16%**	**15%**	**8%**	**23%**
Median		**1.2**	**1.0**	**9.2**	**8.0**	**17.1**	**14.8**	**29.8%**	**10.2%**	**13.0%**	**6.2%**	**1.1%**	**20%**	**14.3%**	**0.8**	**20%**	**15%**	**13%**	**7%**	**22%**

Sources: FactSet; company reports; author estimates.

KEY INDUSTRY METRICS

CONSTRUCTION AND MINING EQUIPMENT

Architecture Billings Index. Each month, the American Institute of Architects (AIA) releases its Architecture Billings Index (ABI), a diffusion index that typically leads nonresidential construction activity in the United States by approximately 9–12 months.

http://www.aia.org/practicing/economics/index.htm

Housing Starts. Each month, the U.S. Census Bureau releases a report on residential housing activity that measures the number of privately owned new houses on which construction has commenced and the number of building permits for new housing units that are issued each month. Normally released around mid-month, the housing report is one of the timeliest indicators of U.S. housing market activity, which over time drives demand for construction machinery. The building permits component of the housing report tends to be a leading indicator of future housing activity.

http://www.census.gov/construction/nrc/

Caterpillar Dealer Statistics. Each month, Caterpillar releases retail sales data for its machines and power systems as reported by its dealers. The sales data cover the most recent three-month rolling period compared with the same period of the prior year and are organized by geography and industry.

http://www.caterpillar.com/investors/financial-information/dealer-statistics

Komatsu Monthly Demand and Orders. Each month, Komatsu publishes the year-on-year monthly growth rates of demand for construction and mining equipment by region, including Japan, North America, Europe, China, Southeast Asia, Oceania, Latin America, CIS, Middle East, and Africa.

http://www.komatsu.com/CompanyInfo/ir/demand_orders/

Construction Spending. Each month, the U.S. Census Bureau releases its report on construction spending in three categories: (1) private construction, which includes single- and multi-family homes; (2) private nonresidential, which includes utility, manufacturing, office, lodging, and religious; and (3) public construction, which includes public schools, highways and streets, military, water, and wastewater. Normally released two months after the reported month, this is one of the least timely government reports.

http://www.census.gov/construction/c30/c30index.html

Mined Commodity Prices. The key driver of demand for mining equipment is mining activity, which, in turn, tends to be highly correlated with the prices of mined commodities, particularly coal, copper, and iron ore prices. Higher commodity prices generally lead to greater equipment usage, which drives increased demand for aftermarket parts and service, replacement demand, and eventually new equipment for mining expansion.

FARM MACHINERY

Unit Sales. Each month, the Association of Equipment Manufacturers (AEM) publishes estimated unit sales of agricultural tractors and combines that were sold during the previous month in the United States and Canada.

http://www.aem.org/MarketInfo/Stats/AgTractorCombine/

Associação Nacional dos Fabricantes de Veículos Automotores (ANFAVEA) also provides similar monthly data for the Brazilian tractor and combine market.

http://www.anfavea.com.br/carta.html

Deere Sales Commentary. Each month, Deere & Co. releases sales commentary for the United States, Canada, and EU27. Incremental information related to industry inventories can be gleaned from these updates.

http://www.deere.com/wps/dcom/en_US/corporate/our_company/investor_relations/presentations_and_webcasts/presentations_and_webcasts.page

Supply and Demand. Each month, the USDA releases its World Agricultural Supply and Demand Estimates (WASDE) report, which forecasts the supply and demand of major crops and livestock. This report is widely considered to be the benchmark against which all other agricultural forecasts are compared.

http://www.usda.gov/oce/commodity/wasde/

Prospective Plantings. Each year in March, the USDA releases its Prospective Plantings report, which forecasts planted acreage for certain major crops, including corn and soybeans. This report has the potential to impact agricultural commodity prices to the extent that the USDA's forecast differs from current market expectations.

http://usda.mannlib.cornell.edu/MannUsda/viewDocumentInfo.do?documentID=1136

Grain Inventories. Each quarter, the USDA releases its Grain Stocks report, which contains the latest estimates on the amount of grain inventories in the United States. Because agricultural commodity prices are largely determined by supply and demand, this report has the potential to impact prices to the extent that inventories differ from current market expectations.

http://usda.mannlib.cornell.edu/MannUsda/viewDocumentInfo.do?documentID=1079

OEM Forecasts. Deere, AGCO, and CNH routinely provide an annual sales outlook for farm machinery by region and periodically update their projections throughout the year. Moreover, Deere regularly provides its outlook for U.S. farm cash receipts, key drivers of demand for farm machinery.

Agricultural Commodity Prices. Corn, soybeans, wheat. Fertilizer prices are also important and correspond to changes in the prices of natural gas.

HEAVY TRUCKS

Trucking Activity. Each month, the American Trucking Associations (ATA) releases its Truck Tonnage Index, which measures changes in the amount of tonnage hauled. The ATA membership sample includes an array of trucking companies, ranging from small fleets to large carriers. A sustained increase in trucking activity is a key driver of demand for heavy trucks.

http://www.truckinginfo.com/list/tag/truck-tonnage-index.aspx

State of the Industry. Each month, Americas Commercial Transportation (ACT) Research publishes its State of the Industry report, which estimates retail sales, new orders, cancellations, net orders, inventory, production, and backlog for the heavy truck industry in North America according to weight class. ACT Research also publishes a separate preliminary report on truck orders at the beginning of each month. These reports are among the timeliest and most comprehensive sources of information for the heavy truck market in North America.

http://www.actresearch.net/

Vehicle Registrations. Each month, the European Automobile Manufacturers' Association (ACEA) reports the number of new commercial vehicle registrations in Europe according to weight class. This report is useful for assessing the current demand environment for heavy trucks in Europe.

http://www.acea.be/collection/statistics

OEM Forecasts. Heavy truck manufacturers and component suppliers routinely provide their outlook for annual truck production volumes by region, and many will periodically update their projections throughout the year. Such companies as PACCAR, Daimler, Eaton, Volvo, Navistar, Cummins, Meritor, Accuride, and Commercial Vehicle Group are among those that have historically provided production forecasts for the industry.

INDUSTRIAL MACHINERY

ISM Index. The ISM Manufacturing Report on Business is one of the timeliest economic indicators that can be used to gauge the health of the industrial machinery segment. Published at 10AM EST on the first business day of each month, it is the first monthly report to focus on activity in the manufacturing sector of the economy during the prior month.

http://www.ism.ws/ismreport/

Regional and country specific PMI Indices that can be used to gauge the health of the manufacturing sector in different parts of the world are published monthly by Markit Group Limited.

http://www.markit.com/en/

Industrial Production and Capacity Utilization. Each month, the Federal Reserve simultaneously releases reports on Industrial Production and Capacity Utilization. The report on industrial production measures the seasonally adjusted real output of the U.S. manufacturing, mining, and utility industries, expressed as a percentage of real output in a base year, currently 2007. The report on capacity utilization measures production levels relative to total production capacity and is also expressed as a percentage of actual output in 2007. These reports are among the more timely government reports on U.S. industrial activity and are normally released on or around the 15th of each month.

http://www.federalreserve.gov/releases/g17/current/

Durable Goods and Factory Orders. Each month, the U.S. Census Bureau releases a preliminary (durable goods) and a final (factory orders) report on manufacturing activity in the United States. The reports provide aggregate data in current dollars on manufacturers' shipments, inventories, and orders for the preceding month organized by industry. Beyond serving as an overall gauge of the health of U.S. manufacturing, the report is particularly useful in assessing recent business conditions for many industries for which data are otherwise difficult to obtain.

http://www.census.gov/manufacturing/m3/

Kennametal Orders. Each month, Kennametal publishes organic order rates for the most recent three-month rolling period compared with the same period of the prior year. The company includes a brief amount of commentary with the report, which often includes management's perspective on current conditions in certain end markets.

http://phx.corporate-ir.net/phoenix.zhtml?c=119933&p=irol-monthlyorders

Parker Hannifin Orders. Each month, Parker Hannifin publishes organic order rates for the most recent three-month rolling period compared with the same period of the prior year. The company reports order rates for four segments: aerospace, cli mate and industrial controls, North America industrial, and international industrial.

http://phx.corporate-ir.net/phoenix.zhtml?c=97464&p=irol-monthlyorders

INDUSTRY RESOURCES

American Institute of Architects (AIA)
1735 New York Ave., NW
Washington, DC 20006-5292
USA
(800) 242-3837
http://www.aia.org/

American Trucking Associations (ATA)
950 North Glebe Road, Suite 210
Arlington, VA 22203-4181
USA
(703) 838-1700
http://www.truckline.com

Americas Commercial Transportation (ACT) Research Co., LLC
4400 Ray Boll Blvd.
Columbus, IN 47203
USA
(812) 379-2085
http://www.actresearch.net/

Associação Nacional dos Fabricantes de Veículos Automotores (ANFAVEA)
Avenida Indianópolis, 496– Moema
São Paulo – SP – Brasil – 04062-900
55 11 2193-7800
http://www.anfavea.com.br/

Association of Equipment Manufacturers (AEM)
6737 West Washington Street
Suite 2400
Milwaukee, WI 53214-5647
USA
(414) 272-0943
http://www.aem.org/

European Automobile Manufacturers' Association (ACEA)
Avenue des Nerviens 85
B-1040 BRUSSELS
32 2 732 55 50
http://www.acea.be/

Institute for Supply Management (ISM)
2055 E. Centennial Circle
P.O. Box 22160
Tempe, AZ 85285-2160
USA
(480) 752-6276
http://www.ism.ws/

Markit Group Limited
711 Executive Blvd
Valley Cottage, NY 10989
USA
(914) 872-2800
http://www.markit.com/en/

Off-Highway Research Limited
35 Great James Street
London WC1N 3HB
UK
44 (0) 20 7404 1128
http://www.offhighway.co.uk/

USDA Economic Research Service
355 E Street SW
Washington, DC 20024-3221
USA
(202) 694-5139
http://www.ers.usda.gov/

U.S. Bureau of Labor Statistics
Postal Square Building
2 Massachusetts Avenue, NE
Washington, DC 20212-0001
USA
(202) 691-5200
http://www.bls.gov/

U.S. Census Bureau
4600 Silver Hill Road
Washington, DC 20233
USA
(301) 763-4636
http://www.census.gov/

U.S. Federal Reserve
20th Street and Constitution Avenue N.W.
Washington, DC 20551
USA
(888) 851-1920
http://www.federalreserve.gov/

WardsAuto
Penton Media
1166 Avenue of the Americas, 10th Fl.
New York, NY 10011
USA
(212) 204-4200
http://wardsauto.com/

World Agricultural Supply and Demand Estimates (WASDE) Report
U.S. Department of Agriculture
1400 Independence Ave., S.W.
Washington, DC 20250
USA
(202) 720-2791
http://www.usda.gov/oce/commodity/wasde/

Yengst Associates
35 Old Ridgefield Road
Wilton, CT 06897
USA
(203) 762-8096
http://www.yengstassociates.com/

Made in the USA
Monee, IL
05 November 2026

67383297R00031